# Gifts of the Magi

## A CHRISTMAS SAMPLER

Gene Clemens

ISBN 978-0-9977956-5-3

Copyright 2021 by Yesteryear Publishing.

All rights reserved. No part of this publication may be reproduced or transmitted in any form or by any means electronic or mechanical, including photocopy, recording, or any information storage and retrieval system now known or to be invented, without permission in writing from the publisher, except by a reviewer who wishes to quote brief passages in connection with a review written for incluion in a magazine, newspaper, or broadcast.

Published in the United States by Yesteryear Publishing.

Books are available at www.amazon.com as well as through the author or publisher:

## Yesteryear Publishing

91 Grandview Road

Hummelstown, PA 17036

www.yesteryearpublishing.org

yesteryearpublishing@gmail.com

717-566-3907

# About the Author

Children and grandchildren cannot possibly know us as we were as children or as vibrant young adults. They cannot relate to our experiences as children, even if those experiences were the foundation for the way we reared them. Thus, this tribute is to my own parents and my views of Christmas through their doing and to my now-adult children who are more like the child I was than they realize, and especially to their children (my grandchildren) who have been creating their own memories of Christmas which Vada and I hope will include us.

Thus this book of my memories of childhood Christmases with my own parents, as well as nearer memories held of my own children and grandchildren, is dedicated to the most important unit any of us will ever have, **Our Family.**

Gene

Dr. Eugene Clemens held an appointment as Professor of Religious Studies at Elizabethtown College in Pennsylvania, is a published author, and, in his own words, "an eternal metaphor." Gene and Vada are the parents of three children and grandparents to seven grandchildren.

# Christmas is all

It is childhood fantasy, beauty, playful spirits, and sweet sentimentality—all wrapped up together in loveliness. In the figure of the benevolent Santa, fully seen only with the fantastical eye of a child, is personified generosity and the cornucopia of awaiting delights. Christmas is also coziness of home, bustle of preparation, the anticipation of celebrations revisited, and stories shared with ones we love.

At its height and culmination, this supreme of all holidays elevates our selfhood to openheartedness and stirs our hopes for universal good will. Its signature of authenticity proclaimed is "Peace to All!" In the vulnerable Child we place our care for the world. In return, we receive the saving gift of hope.

Permit this small gift, dear friend, to carry the fairest treasures of the season. They are from within me, the accumulated tastings and dreams of Christmas. In a larger respect, they are representative of the commonality we receive in all our shared traditions. May my tokens make their way into your home, as added brightness to your festive trimmings.

# Table of Contents

Behold the Star of our Dark Night  -  Christmas 1981 .......................... 9

My Moravian Star  -  Christmas 1984 ...................................... 11

Christmas: The Celebration of Incarnation  -  Christmas 1983 ................ 13

Gifts from the Magi ...................................................... 15

Images of Christmas: Fragrance from a Potpourri .......................... 19

Two Christmas Melodies  -  For then and for now ......................... 25

Remember the Child  -  Christmas 1984 .................................. 29

The Spirit of the Christmas Child  -  Christmas 1982 ...................... 31

The Season of Christmas  -  Christmas 1976 .............................. 33

What is Christmas?  -  Christmas 1979 ................................... 35

The First Gift of Christmas is The Gift We Give Christmas ................... 37

A Tinkertoy Windmill: Memory of an early Christmas ...................... 39

Christmas Cookies ...................................................... 45

Christmas Cards in a Garret Keep ....................................... 49

The Night We Almost Missed Christmas Eve Service ....................... 55

Dear Dad  -  Christmas 1982 ............................................ 59

# My Moravian Star

Each of us has a star to raise,
So that the world may see.

The star was there at our birth,
Spark of divine from which we came.

Then, through the ardor of our heart
We fashioned the star of our life.

The star expresses what our spirit creates,
The love and wisdom and beauty.

Before our body settles to peaceful rest,
We raise the star of our spirit.

We do not vainly raise it, for it is our tribute
to the Eternal Spirit,

Shining so brightly in the heaven of birth,
To which we all in time shall return.

Christmas 1984

# Christmas:
## The Celebration of Incarnation

Christmas is the season to celebrate our incarnation.

We look at the new born child and exclaim that it is right to celebrate and We celebrate by immersing ourselves in the beauty of the season and the pleasures of sensuous delight.

Let it be a time of feasting and pageantry, of glitter and enchantment, of dazzling colors and joyous sounds.

The more we allow the presence of the divine spirit to refine our appreciation of the sensible, the higher we raise the carol of our rejoicing.

# Gifts From the Magi

I sit enraptured by longing thoughts of Christmas. Before me on this pensive day are tokens of Christmases past: a nineteenth century copy of Dickens' A Christmas Carol, a small box of balsam pine incense, and a bayberry candle—gold, frankincense, and myrrh. These are treasures as worthy as any the Magi ever could bring. Each is a vessel of sweet sentiment, delicious memory, and delightful imagery, pleasantly conveying me to the enchantment of childhood.

As my fingers touch the book, festive scenes from throughout the ages flash before my eyes. I hear joyous declarations, quickened to life by the merriment of congeniality and resplendence of the season. The full exuberance echoes the exultation of angels. I see travelers at a wayside inn, toasting friendship with hot wassail before the warmth of a flickering Yule fire. This scene fades, giving way to the dim outlines of bundled figures wending their way through dancing snowflakes in the return home from an afternoon shopping, strains of carols still lilting in the growing darkness of evening. With increasing frequency lights appear in the windows of welcoming dwellings, revealing rooms in decoration for the holidays.

One faint whiff from the box of balsam incense draws me into a rapturous trance. I am led into chambers of Christmas trees past, the air sweet with the scent of pine needles warmed by lights glowing in the stillness of night. I am lying prone, peering up at the glistening colors of lights as they beam their magic into my wide-eyed imagination. Gaily wrapped presents enveloping the foot of the tree evoke fantasies of Santa's workshop, then playful babes in Toyland. Expectantly I await the arrival of the Nutcracker, to lead the awakening toys in a martial parade of precise cadence. I am willfully captured by them, to be borne in their march to never-ever-land, beyond Raggedy Ann's grotto of strawberry-flavored icicles to the very gates of the Snow Queen's palace.

The glint of the bayberry candle flame catches the corner of my eye as my fingers absorb the velvety touch of its warming wax. The gleam, the touch, and the spicy fragrance transport my imagination to another far gone room of life. And, yet another candle. To the Christmas Eve of that childhood year came my gift-bearing grandfather from afar, not unlike Santa. His mighty form appeared in the doorway of that night, his smile as widely generous as my esteem for him was deep. It was as though he brought gifts from the larger world I longed to know. Readily I believed he was brought to our house aloft, riding upon the brisk air currents of winter, a Magi following a guiding star. Among the gifts he bestowed was a genuine bayberry candle from New England. I stroked it imploringly, as though it were a soothsayer's talisman, just as I now invoke its power. Years ago, that candle was an Aladdin's lamp, with a genie to guide me to far-away, exotic lands. Now it carries me back to cherished scenes of youth. In the airy spirits of the season I have circled the earth and have delved to the depths of memory. Then, it was Santa's delivery of gifts. Now, internalizing what once was given, I have become my own treasure-bearer.

What a joy is Christmas! The season is replete with so many elements of goodness, brought together by a holy spirit of harmony, the very essence of life's longing. I would not wish to live without it. What more can one say, without becoming effusive? The tongue would speak in eulogy, so to bring to heart its

joys. Though such grandeur is not fully containable in words, allow me to laud its magnificence and to sing its praises. No definition of Christmas is necessary. Just well-chosen memories are sufficient to open the flood gates of a vast delectable emotional reservoir. But first, a few strokes of magnification.

Seasonally, Christmas is the bright warmth of colorful festivity, afore the onset of winter's dark cold. It is a merry Christmas! Yet, graciously added to that are the finest gifts fantasy and good will can bestow. Christmas is the holiday in tribute to the reason by which we exist. In its celebration we dramatically act out the better parts of our lives. By virtue of this prompting we reaffirm what is enduring, as we transition into the dreary, numbing period of the year.

Into this pageant converge impersonations of quintessential moments we have gleaned from life, the gems of existence we most value. In bringing together and intensifying the finest aspects of this world, we create and participate in a higher, more perfect state of being. Thus, it is a time of glorification, a ceremony of gladness reawakening and reliving the presence of the Holy. Within its encircling domain dwell both exuberance and hushed reverence, alternating as in duet. "Santa is Coming" in concert with "Silent Night." We wax serene in heightened awareness before the source of our jubilation, the Eternal Principle of Light and Love.

# IMAGES OF CHRISTMAS;

# FRAGRANCE FROM A POTPOURRI

*In exploring the vast cornucopia of my Christmas memories, I acknowledge indebtedness to multiple sources and many benefactors. Beyond the obvious ones of church, family, commerce, and school, I have discovered numerous less manifest derivations, making Christmas a complex blend of diverse ingredients—a grand piquant potpourri of scents and a spectacular collage of images.*

*It seems probable that the mixture and flavor, the pattern and configuration of each person's Christmas is as unique and discrete as the peculiar experience of every individual. Yet these diversities converse congenially with one another, overlaying the meaning of each other in song. This is true of all primal human commemorations, so let us all be directed and absorbed into Christmas as the supreme expression of life's joyousness.*

Christmas is not just one piece, not only one thread or one cloth. Rather, it is interwoven as an emblem of all that we delight in and is displayed as a rich tapestry. By its authority, all who wish to share in the pageantry are invited to bring the finest of their trade. There are many sources and much variety and none should seek to be the master, for Christmas is both a minstrel show and a morality play, a tale for the children and a dance for the free spirit. This high festival is the occasion for all openhearted persons to be welcomed, each enlarging and amplifying upon the other, mutually supportive.

It is not a competition seeking to distract from or negating other gifts. Rather, the story of this advent of winter jubilation is one grand, all-inclusive tale, a compendium of narrations from out the large company of joyous carolers who may have various names and multiple costumes. Some will sing in joy of God incarnate, others will celebrate the immanence of the divine in beauty and love. Some will note the purity of liberation's light, others the brilliance of truth revealed. Individuality, the nurturing parent, will intone an affectionate lullaby for the child; the merrymaker will toast the good fortune of comrade fellowship, while the artist will laud the ideal of form and grace. From many songs there is but one hymn and, while many stanzas enhance the melody, there is only one chorus, "Peace on Earth."

I receive gratefully all the images of Christmas, yet of several I am especially fond, for they have been leading actors on my stage for the holiday. Beyond the nativity narrative and the fable of Santa Claus, no one single story has had a more prominent place in the enactment than that of Dickens' A Christmas Carol. I have relished every line, each scene, and all the unrestrained sentimentalism filling the pages. A portion of each Christmas season is spent walking the fog-chocked lanes of old London Town, excitedly anticipating nephew Fred's "Merry Christmas!" and redoubtable reply of Scrooge's "Humbug!"

The annual reading of the story is an unquestioned necessity, whether in recitation to my children, as earlier, or in private litany, as of late. Because the tale reassures me that not even so grasping and covetous a soul as Scrooge's can go unaffected by the cordiality of the season, my Christmas is partially attired in the top hat and scarf, bonnet and bustling skirt of the Dickens' era. Small paned shop windows emit warm candlelight as Bob Cratchit makes his way home to his awaiting family. In a dreary, cold chamber a wretched old man awaits the arrival of three spirits and the redemption of his soul. The picture blurs and then blends into a cold, snowy winter spectacle.

Good King Wenceslaus, from the window of his regal comfort, sees a poor man gathering winter fuel. With this rekindled sense of charity, I realize it is again time to drop in the Red Kettle a generous portion of my own good fortune. This is the way I wanted Christmas to be, for my family and all people.

Since the days of college, I have found another charming series of images to add to the holiday repertoire, Amahl and the Night Visitors. More oriental and intriguing in mood, this story belongs in my well-kept treasure box, along with a bright star and a silent night. Timeless in its philosophical dimensions, Amahl transports me simultaneously to ancient Palestine and feudal Europe. Somehow they fit together in my sense of where mystic revelation occurs. Merged are the tradition of the Wise Men, the Magi, and the miracle of self-giving. Is there any greater wisdom to Christmas than that? Thus, shepherd and peasant costumes rightly appear in my holiday theater, garments of perennial personages bearing the eternal truths of our existence. Without this element of solemnity, the holiday would drown in the superficiality of wonton merrymaking.

Also very special in my personal collection of Christmas accessories are the strains of the German carol. To be sure, it must partially be due to the prominence given to the Tannenbaum and snow. Yet, more than that, in the carols of German origin I find an almost unexcelled tone of serenity, tranquility, and peacefulness. When sung by the seraphic quality of children voices some of these carols ascend to near celestial states of pure bliss. Incomparable is the quiescence of Stille Nacht (Silent Night). Not to be reserved for Christmas Eve, this carol remains a supreme expression of the reverence due to the nativity, its veneration rising to that of a hymn.

One rainy day, in the manner of making a personal pilgrimage, I found myself at the Austrian birthplace of this remarkable carol where I paid my respects in the small chapel erected on the site of its first singing. I arrived as a shepherd and went forth enriched by the experience.

Two similarly toned carols, both lilting and stirring, also grace my Christmas observances. In the still night air I can hear the clear strains of Süßer die Glocken nie klingen (Never did the Bells ring sweeter). When the first delicate flakes of snow begin to descend, the melody transposes to Leise rieselt der Schnee (Softly falls the Snow). These remind me of my ethnic origins, at the same time providing reminders from all the grand traditions of this holiday potpourri.

# Two Christmas Melodies

## ...For then and for now

The repertoire of Christmas carols is so vast that I offer gratitude for them all, for how can there be Christmas without melody. I relish both the singing and the listening. I thrive on them. Without music filling the air, the days of Christmas would be almost as devoid of a setting, as winter is without snow in areas accustomed to a white Christmas.

From the first plaintive notes of *Oh, Come Emmanuel*, through the hushed strains of *Silent Night*, to the exuberant exclamation of *We Wish You a Merry Christmas*, I am carried along on currents of emotional elevation. Music can, indeed, elevate us to heights of both sentimentality and spirituality. While every holiday seems to have its songbook, never is melody more called upon than at Christmas time.

When I was a child, nothing could stir my anticipation to greater intensity, than to hear the song, *Santa Claus is Coming to Town*. Together with Clement Moore's *A Visit from St. Nicholas*, the lyrics of these songs prepared me for the glorious morning when all presents were to be opened.

As the days neared that explosive point in time, the building excitement within became uncontainable, nearly uncontrollable. Because of the warning lyric of "Oh, you better...," my sister and I were on our good behavior, making parental control nearly unneeded.

♪ It mattered not the least that I never saw Santa Claus in person, other than in a department store. Because of the song I knew exactly what would happen, so I followed Santa all the way from the North Pole and back again, in the most vivid of imagining. The elves, the reindeer, the sack of toys, the chimney and fireplace, they were all there! Had I not experienced them with certainty, in every delightful detail? Even though we had no fireplace, whether or not snow fell, I would not be denied. Fantasy took flight with the reindeer. Even the presents I opened required special handling, even after I suspected my parents' hands were somehow involved in the packaging.

I do believe I remember the first time ever I heard the song. I was but a few years old and my mother had taken me with her uptown to do Christmas shopping. We entered what then seemed to me to be an enormous building. My eyes were probably agog as we walked from one section of the store to another. This new world was awesomely colorful and attractive, filled with an endless array of fascinating goods.

We descended stairs and in the darkening surroundings everything seemed more compressed. A most pleasant aroma hung in the air, a mixture of new cloth and sweet candy. All of this increasing euphoria induced a sense of well-being. I felt fully happy, content to have my hand in my mother's. Then, I would inevitably hear this unforgettable melody coming from somewhere above: "You better watch out; you better not cry; You better not pout; I'm telling you why.....

In spite of the dire injunction, it was such good fortune to begin life in this way, with a note of happiness. Even today, each time I listen to that song, I am swept over by an indescribable wave of delight, in touch with the simple state of childhood.

♪ Just as there are songs for children and for adults with childhood still in them, there are songs for adults, requiring many Christmases for children to understand them. The song, "I'll be Home for Christmas," has long had a cherished place in my heart. However, it was not until the Christmas season after the family home of thirty-five years was sold that the song's most poignant impression was made.

My father had died the spring before, surviving my mother by eight years. The house he and I had largely built was now a Christmas home for another family and I was traveling all day to spend a second holiday with my sister living in the same town in which we had grown up.

By the time I had crossed the Indiana line darkness had come and a light snow had begun to fall. As my car drew me nearer to that very special town of my past, each dancing flake carried me further back in time, to other Christmases…and my heart was heavy as I reviewed in my mind the many holidays spent in that home. There were the Christmases of college and those of early marriage and later my family and those of my sister and brother gathered for reunion at Christmas. It was quite truly, "Over the river and through the woods, to Grandmother's house we go," excitement building by the mile. We would arrive with good spirits in heart and packages in arms.

Late night talks followed Christmas Eve candlelight service, as sugarplums danced in another generation's wee little heads. Frenzied present opening was followed by a sumptuous dinner, always a little later than planned, with an intermission for toy playing, of course, permitted. All of this passed reverently through my musings, my feelings growing more fragile by the minute.

I entered the outskirts of the town and was grasped by a powerful urge to drive past that home of yore. As the longing grew, I placed "I'll be home for Christmas" into the tape deck. When I turned the corner from Main Street onto the side street of my childhood home, my heart was pounding and my breathing became heavy. There, through the light snow and evening's growing darkness, serving as a faint apparition in the dim illumination of a street lamp, at a turn in the road, appeared my parents' house. As I passed by it, every inhibition melted in me and tears flowed down my cheeks. Gradually the emotional enormity subsided into a warm contentment that the home ever was at all.

I then slowly made my way to my sister's house, but the intensity of that encounter with Christmases past was even slower in passing. In an extraordinary manner a truth that I already had known was confirmed. It is most assuredly true that I will always be home for Christmas, even if it be only in my dreams. Although the song had been written for troops far away from home, through the tears of my own nostalgia I found a place beside those men, owning that valuing of life unites all of us. Time can take away the place, but the treasured sentiment of what once was can last a lifetime. Thus is the story of life itself.

I know both sides now. I feel the joy in the child at Christmas time, for I was that child. And, after many years, I better understand the occasional misty eyes I saw in grownups when I was a child. They have become my own.

Remember the child,
    dear Father Christmas,
The sweet, tender child
    cradled in us all.

Call us again
    this festive season
To that marvelous,
    innocent wonderland.

In reawakening to
    the joy of youth
May we care for
    the Child in us all.

**Christmas 1984**

# The Spirit of the Christmas Child

What we most desire as a Christmas present is the Christmas of our childhood. What we experience in the Christmases of adulthood is the revisiting of those wonder-filled moments of youth, when fantasy was unblemished by the harsh realities of a world forgetful of the heart.

We like the presence of small children at Christmas, for they bring to living form the spirit of our dear memories. We relish imaginatively extending ourselves into their gleeful exuberance. The indwelling child is so readily excited and delighted by the things of Christmas, an enthusiasm easily worn away by time.

Let us shed a tear at the loss of the Christmases forever in the past, yet may we also with each new Christmas rekindle that spirit of joyousness and entreat a small child to guide us

Christmas 1982

# The Season of Christmas

*The season of Christmas is too delicious to be limited to one day.*

As the spirit of festivity and merriment, bursting forth to celebrate its own existence, it must be sung to, luxuriated in, doted over, or even occasionally abandoned—throughout the season's many days—in order to embrace it fully.

One must pour out upon the season the spirit's inner exultation, the heightening, and the refining of all.

Attending with this fullest and richest joy, one then can better understand the limitless and inexplicable wealth of Christmas as the soul's supreme rhapsody of living, fulfilling its reason for being.

It is seemly that God's manifesto should be associated with this time, for what better way than this to designate the holy intensity of spirit with Christmas's supreme rhapsody of living, fulfilling its reason for being.

**Christmas 1976**

# What is Christmas?

A
kaleidoscopic tumbling of lovely sights,
confectionary swirling of emotional delights?

The
sugar plums, sleigh bells, an entourage of fanciful tales, sweet scents, splendid colors, and the cheerful sounds of the season—all blended into one mélange.

The
warm glow of a fireplace
crackle of wrapping paper
crunch of snow under foot
joyous voice of carolers
gleeful squealing of children.

The
taste of cinnamon candy canes
embrace of friends a the door
sweetness of cookies in the air
magic of a lighted tree by dark
twinkling of multicolored lights.

The
glistening of snow upon tree tops
tingling touch of falling snowflakes
helpful bustle of dinner preparation
glide of skate blades upon smooth ice
squeak of old sled runners on new snow.

And the solemn stillness of a candlelight service

For this one yearns passionately. To take it all up entire into oneself, undifferentiated, and to be filled with its overwhelming, overflowing sense of wellbeing ...
this is what Christmas is. In it we are both the blessing and the blessed.

# The First Gift of Christmas is The Gift We Give Ourselves

There is a treasure box in each of us, locked and hidden away for most of the year. In it have been stored all of the sentimental delights of Christmas past.

Before the wrappings are laid aside, all the endeared sights, sounds, scents, and tastes of that particular Christmas are tucked away in a splendid chest of riches.

That treasure trove increases in wealth over the years. Each holiday season requires only a hearing or a seeing, of a song or a scene, to place that precious parcel of memory once again within our emotional stream.

Dear Friend, may this be the first gift of your Christmas season, the opening of this remarkable box, which lies, awaiting, within. From out of it you will give the wealth of Christmas to others.

Joyfulness from my gift box to yours.

# A Tinkertoy Windmill:
## Memory of an Early Christmas

Out from Santa's sack tumbled memorable toys into my wishful childhood. A rubber dolly, somehow to be named "Dicky Boy" and with whom I took naps on the floor, is the earliest of my recollections, with many modestly priced though gratefully received presents followed in annual succession.

There were drums, toy tractors, a kaleidoscope, a sled, a miniature steam engine that ran on alcohol, a microscope, Lincoln logs, an Erector set, and a play doctor's satchel with candy pills and a rubber-hosed stethoscope.

Camouflaged among the toys were numerous articles of winter clothing, the most forgivable being a tease-worthy one-piece zippered snowsuit—which turned out to be marvelously warm—even in the snow. Matching knitted mittens were attached by an entangling length of yarn. Later, when the fingers of friends were frozen and snow worked its way to their midriffs, I remained snug—privately realizing my mother's attention to detail.

Memorable for my twelfth Christmas was the electric train I had so long coveted and by my early teens adventure books came in welcomed regularity—Nancy Drew from my aunt Trudy and Hardy Boys from a good friend. However, the automatic Red Ryder BB gun I was convinced I needed for my tour of the Western plains, in spite of repeated hints, never came by way of the Christmas tree. Neither was there ever the Nutcracker of lore and dance, nor the tin soldiers of marching fame—though the tunes still play in my mind whenever the names are mentioned. Yet my toys did come alive under the spell of tree lights by night and I early received an ever-so-equivalent drum major for the Christmas grand parade: a Tinkertoy windmill!

For some years a confusion prevailed as to whether our presents were to be opened in the darkness of Christmas Eve or in the dim early light of Christmas Morn. Sometimes—mainly when our grandfather would come bursting in with presents on Christmas eve—we did open these already much handled treasures. While the premature disclosure did seem a bit disrespectful of Santa's traditional role in the pageant, the arrival of our would-be Santa grandfather served as a sufficient justification. Additionally, we rationalized, "Did not the Three Wise Men bring gifts by night?" With more advanced theology that question arose again later, but in this Christmas of early childhood all was quite readily accepted.

The house of those years on Lafayette Street was small by adult measure, but more than ample for a child's world of fantasy. Upon entrance through a centered front door, windows presented themselves to the right, under which the couch ordinarily sat. An open, spindle staircase claimed the left. The walls and ceiling were coated with a coarse, patterned plaster, fashionable in the 1920s. Lighting was provided by two small fixtures of bulbs set in plastic candles, artificial wax beginning to drip down their sides. On the far side from the door, to accompany the touch of Spanish décor, was a gracefully rounded archway, the corridor beyond which admitted one to a bathroom on the right and the kitchen on the left, where we usually had our meals. Straight ahead, somewhat like an inner sanctum awaiting hesitant curiosity, was the dining room. I valued that misnamed chamber as it suggested more of a Peter Pan ephemera than middle class formality.

I would usually take naps on its kitchen floor, whispering ever so softly to my imaginary friend before we both slipped off into dreamland. Before the lace curtained windows stood my mother's productive sewing machine with which for years she made most of my sister's and my clothes. I can still hear the hum of the motor and staccato of its needle, as I whiled away pleasant hours in play with this reassuring sound in a secure world. On rainy days I would stand at the windows, oriented as they were to the west, my eyes just about even with the sill, and look out upon the neighbor yards, yearning to explore what lay beyond, mesmerized by the strange cooing of mourning doves on the telephone lines.

The room also possessed an intriguing closet, replete with artifacts from the vast world I so longed to visit: literature on the Great Lakes Exhibition of 1934, brochures of Cleveland, postcards from Niagara Falls, and my first encounter with a brontosaurus as the emblematic picture of Sinclair Oil. All this paved a way to an adventuresome future. Yet, for all that the dining room had to offer, on this particular occasion it was the living room in which the magic took place.

The open staircase led to the two bedrooms on the second floor. My parents slept in the front bedroom and my sister and I shared the back bedroom. That particular Christmas Eve (1938 I surmise) the two of us were put to bed shortly after dark, earlier because of anticipating Santa. Though I recall little of it, I want to believe my sister and I had dreams of Toyland that night—as we had heard the melody on the radio. In the faintest of morning light one of us stirred and awakened the other. Unable to sustain our own hushed voices in the rising tide of excitement, we stole out of bed and slipped on our bunny shoes, furry house slippers with a nose on the toe and eyes beneath king ears at the instep. Quietly opening our door and stealthily passing our parents' room, we took the first gingerly steps upon the stairs with my unrestrained eagerness leading the way.

We had gone but a few steps downward, when suddenly our eyes were met by a most dazzling sight. (The night before after we had been put to bed and had fallen asleep, our dear father had moved the couch and in its place now stood a fully trimmed tree.) The room was filled with the sweet aroma of pine needles—a measure I may not have noted then, yet, a scent which in later life would almost invariably take me back to that gleeful moment. The tree nearly reached the ceiling, towering over us as we rushed toward it. Covered with lights, balls, and tinsel, this adored tree possessed all the majesty and magic our childish hearts could ever have hoped for. Even now, so many years later, in my imagination I can still see two sweet and happy children, sister and brother, standing enchanted before a glittering tree on Christmas morning. Thus, a lifetime image was etched in my mind, forever to keep alive the meaning of Christmas for the perennial child in us all.

In front of the tree, to the left, as though waiting the night just for my arrival, stood the TinkerToy Windmill. I knew it was for me. Too young to understand the intricacies of advanced engineering—at that point I had only advanced to the stage of wooden blocks, I stood for a brief moment in innocent admiration. There would have been other presents to be opened, but they are now lost to memory. It was the windmill that held my fascination, a new world discovered. I was oblivious to all other activities, lost in a state of blissful detachment, as only a freely imaginative child can be. At first, I played with the windmill as though it was already in operation, hesitant to alter it for fear of not being able to reassemble it. However, with the help of my father, I boldly set off on a venture into endless creative possibility.

From the standpoint of grownups, these scant pieces of wood were just that, mere pieces of wood. Yet to me (and children throughout the world) these physical properties, named "toys," were, and ever shall be, escorts into extraordinary dimensions. As an adult I have found other more sophisticated media into the land of potentiality, but I will never forget my first opening into that wonderland—a toy windmill being my challenge, my guide, and my companion.

As I climbed the stairway to bed Christmas night, I paused for a moment to look down on a most delightful sight:

Below was my Tinkertoy Windmill

in the soft glow of a gleaming Christmas tree

and I knew there would be a promising tomorrow.

# THE CHRISTMAS COOKIES

When I was young my uncle bore the affectionate nickname of "Cookie". That was not so much because he gave them to us when he was older as that he took them with abandon when a boy. He loved and lived for cookies. I, too, could have been named Cookie, although maybe not so craving in need or so daring in the acquiring. There were scarcely any cookies I would not gladly eat. Each, and then another, was devoured with unmixed pleasure and complete satisfaction. It was not as though I had no discernment in taste. I was fully aware of the entire range of flavor and took note of each, favoring some over the others, but turning almost none aside. No, it was because I loved cookies, because I was a connoisseur of all such offerings of the baker's art. As the flower is the crown of creation, the signet of nature's beauty, to me the cookie was the epitome of delectability.

If I was the consummate cookie consumer, my mother was the principal supplier. Because we rarely bought cookies at the grocery store, most of my early varieties came from my mother and jars of relatives. The only ones I remember from the store were Dutch Windmill cookies, sprinkled on top with sliced almonds, and pungent ginger snaps, both well regarded by my father. During the course of most of the year the staple cookies were crunchy oatmeal and chewy peanut butter, the latter given its distinctive signature by a crisscross press of a fork. Special cookies were gingerbread, large sugar, and hickory nut. Make-shift cookies were graham crackers with confectionary sugar filling. How I delighted in cookies. If sugarplums have a fairy, I thought that at least cookies should have a brownie. That delectable morsel, however, along with chocolate chip cookies, was not a frequent treat in my childhood of the late 'Thirties. Chocolate was much too luxurious for the meager budget of my parent's first years of marriage. Those fineries came later. In the dreams of youth my ultimate expectation was to come upon the wicked witch's gingerbread house, deep in the forest, and enjoy an endless nibbling holiday. Not even the thought of witches seemed to deter my predilection.

Then came Christmas, the high season of cookies. To be sure, other sweets entered into this abundant time of the year. My father would rave about Clara Cotherman's homemade chocolates, each individually dipped and exactingly wrapped. From Sunday school came the annual box of hard candies, nicely equipped with string handles. Back home in our front room was to be found a large bowel of traditional candies, the ribbon candy in the continuous 'S' shape being the most interesting, the ones with questionable tasting raspberry centers the least bearable. I do remember a Christmas when my father attempted his own version of hard candy, cooked pure sugar flavored with essence of wintergreen, spearmint, and sassafras, each dyed in its appropriate color. On her side of sweet treats, our mother made divinity fudge with black walnuts, but that usually went with her to the Women's Missionary Society. I can honestly say, neither met my approval nor was worth the bother. The so-called divinity fudge was so sweet as to put your teeth on edge, scarcely what a child preferring quantity over daintiness is looking for. I thought, if the angels needed pure sugar for their wings and halos, I would leave the fudge to them. I did not outright dislike my father's candies, rather regarded them as an acquired taste, like the horehound candy from his youth, and left them alone, as long as other candies were available. I chose to be kind to his preference, for I suspected he was living out the best of all too sparse Christmases of his early years. Sometimes peanut brittle or taffy would emerge from the kitchen, family fun in the making but less enjoyable in the consuming. Quite certainly, there were many sweets for the holidays, but no rivals. Supreme was the cookie.

In the order of service that is the Christmas cookie, two dimensions of the communion are to be reviewed: Making and Eating. Each aspect was definitely an integral part of what it meant to observe Christmas. One Christmas I read a story in a children's magazine, which has ever after set the scene for the ritual of cookie-making. Our family did other Christmas preparations together—bringing in and trimming the tree, readying the house, and setting the table, but the togetherness I cherished the most was making cookies. The story told of a mother and her two small children, sister and brother. Festivity was in the air and everyone was in holiday spirit. Anticipation, joyous as a carol, filled this home on a bright, sunny day the week before Christmas. The mother took the children to the kitchen and together they made cut-out cookies, she lovingly and patiently bearing with their inexperience. When the father came home they all had several cookies and a glass of milk. I longed for the same love and harmony in my family. I think it to be true, I have been enacting that ideal scene ever since. You can eat a cookie anytime, to celebrate the sweetness of the season. But, the making is to be communal.

From our German heritage came two cookies, the springerle and the pfeffernuss. Flavored with anise the heavy springerle dough was rolled on a board with a carved pin, leaving designs and lines for cutting. Alternatingly freshly baked soft, unbitably rock hard, then eatably soft again, it depended upon whether you wanted to teeth babies—and we did ours—or preferred slowly munching on a rather pleasant piece of bakery, as to when you took the cookie out of the tin container. My mother would usually put a cut apple in the tin to keep the contents a little on the moist side. As to the pfeffernuss, literally "peppernut," I prefer to reserve judgment, except to say, it is a travesty against the concept of cookie. Highly spiced—I think it was the ground cardamom and excessive pepper I most disapproved of—this small, round chunk of indigestible dough was, I assumed, misplaced in the company of well-behaved cookies. Sort of like Charlie Brown's Christmas tree, you could only love it for what it was not. Yet, why linger on the disagreeable, when the cut-cookie, as the Germans say of Christmas, "stands at the door."

Christmas would not be complete without the cut-cookie. Made of a sweet, floury dough, our cookies were cut in the shape of Christmas trees, Santas, stars, and bells. Painted with milk and sprinkled with colored sugar, these darling of the baker's art came out of the oven a bit cakey within but crispy on the outside. Of course, the trees were green and the Santas red, to bear the colors of the season, but the others would be yellow and blue, to suggest light over Bethlehem and the clarity of carols. My delight was in the sugary cut-cookie, yet my favorite was possibly the filled-cookie. Made of the same dough but rolled thinner, the two round cut pieces were placed one upon the other, after cherry, date, or blueberry filling was added. Then the edges were crimped with a fork and a cross marked on the top. Like any imaginative child, I doted on anything miniature and regarded these cookies as a tiny pie, my very own. Somehow the word "tart" became associated with this specialty, adding a further touch of scenery from the English tradition. I would fancy myself at a medieval fair, securing tarts for the Christmas festival.

What a colorful array were these sweet tidbits of the season, whether on the kitchen counter or on a plate awaiting devouring. Partly out of Mrs. Claus' oven and entirely within the keeping of the holiday, one bite would sweep me into a dreamy trance and assure me of imagined realities. It was, indeed, a eucharist, a partaking of the essential goodness of life. Allotted sparingly in the days before, the Great Cookie Feast began on Christmas Day. Oh, how scrumptious the consuming! But the celebration of the divine cookie continued further. Pleasantly I recall sitting at the kitchen table, an afternoon or two after the day of high communion, splendidly dining on six or eight cookies my mother had bestowed upon me, accompanied by a glass of milk. The wafer and wine of Cookiedom! The first was nibbled in commemoration of the holy day, but the subsequent ones were devoured in gleeful abandon, usually soaked by a dunking in the disappearing milk. The partaking of these remnants of Christmas left me content in the knowledge that it had been a goodly season and in due course another such fine occasion would come.

A milk toast in tribute to you, illustrious Christmas Cookie! Even more than the abundant measure of the Christmas Dinner, you have aided me in keeping well the meaning of the season. I await your return, when once again you come 'round.

"Here come the cookies!!"

# Christmas Cards in a Garret Keep

The second story of the house of my childhood was not full-size. Rather, its "upstairs" had been built with low, slanted ceilings and windows only at the gable ends. In my child's view this shortfall was amply compensated for by cubbyholes running along the eave sides of the two bedrooms located there. Small doors, about three feet high, allowed for my sister and me to enter these darkened, somewhat anxiety-inducing, hideaways, scented with mustiness and saturated with intrigue. To our delight, however, each small doorway was an entrance into imaginative play and mysteries of the past—the only use we had of an attic. The small-sized doors and stooped interior were all the more suggestive of storyland wee people—gnomes and elves—that I believed dwelt in the gloomy recesses. Every unusual sound emanating from the dark interior only confirmed my belief. Though our parents managed to enter the area on infrequent occasions to store items, the smallness of space seemed to indicate these passageways were especially made for the use of children. (Oh, yes, at night strange creatures also lurked under my bed.)

*The adjacent photo provides a visual of a garret attic with storage area access. It is not the Clemens' attic. Note that there is space for furniture, windows, and head room.*

 The more fantastical aspects aside for the moment, among the many tangible discoveries I made in venturing into my family's past was a box of old Christmas cards. The large container included cards my parents had received in those unknowable years before my arrival into this world, etched cards my father made in return, and sheaves of sample cards from discarded catalogues. The latter cache had come from the printing plant where my father worked. Looking back, I marvel at how these simple images with so little embellishment could take me far into a lifetime of permanent holiday magnificence.

I spent much time sequestered away here in this garret keep, peering through these token symbols. Here, I suspect, is where the fundamental outlines of my Christmas memories were sketched upon my impressionable childhood. Finer details have been added in more mature years and recent cards have been only ornaments upon my first impressions.

Borrowing upon the evidence of Christmases which were there before me, I constructed within my imagination a new Christmas of grand scale, excitedly anticipating the Christmas to come. Each Christmas was all the richer for it, adding a new layer of sentiment with each occurrence. I, the artist of my own imaginative kingdom, sat in the middle of the realm—in the attic of all time.

Scenes on the cards were the prosaic, less spell-binding tokens of the season—beribboned bells ringing, sleigh bells jingling, ice skaters gliding, snowy New England village windows showing, fireplaces glowing—and I received them all quite willingly if only for their intended holiday spirit.

However, the scenes which remained most indelible were of a different magnitude, powerful in their command over my imaginary flight. These conjured spirits to guide me on my wondrous ventures even while banal in appearance. The printed scenario which was most mysterious and eerie in my mind was the midnight blue card with a radiant star of gold. The three Wise Men on camelback were silhouetted in one corner and the still-lying-ahead Bethlehem in the other. Though by scriptural account the Wise Men came later, these personages from the East—representing the essences of gold, frankincense, and myrrh—set the stage for the current view of the silent night of Christmas Eve. For me the awe and spell of this sacred nocturne is the transcendental height of the holiday. Universal in reach, peace and good spontaneously flow from the heart when swept to these heights.

A card bearing the lighted Christmas tree was next in the pile, its illumination intimating the light of the star and its ornamentation heralding the colorful festivities of Christmas Day. There also was the card of a manger scene, but that seemed somewhat more a part of the night than of the day. From the evidence of the cards—darkened stable, shepherds awed by the radiant light of angels—I assumed Jesus was born in the night before Christmas Day.

In addition to the religion-themed cards, there were, of course, many cards featuring Santa Claus. Arriving between the night and the day, the "jolly old elf" provided an interlude between the two, leaving delights for the morning. I sometimes wondered if Santa was just another aspect of God's incarnation, with the message being that the enjoyment of creation is proper and right, that it is all right to be a child. Subsequently, I have refused to regard the subject otherwise.

I positively adored the cards with scenes of Santa's workshop, child-like elves hastily readying presents for the sleigh ride, and was entirely captivated by the spirit of Santa's generosity. I thrilled at glimpses of him alighting on snowy rooftops and somehow slipping down chimneys, with overflowing sack and a "belly, like a bowl full of jelly," to place presents under the tree. Yet the image which delighted me most was the card with

Santa waving in greeting, "ere he flew out of sight, Merry Christmas to all, and to all a good night!"

Viewing the cards was a grand invocation for the festivities of the next day and served as a benediction for the whole season—at least for twelve days. The images on the cards had various cultural and geographic origins, but in the receptive, innocent imagination of this child they all melted together into one grand conglomeration—with stars and mangers coming from the East and the Saint Nicholas of Greece mutating into the Santa Claus of Europe. There in our garret keep all had become one in me.

How many marvelous hours I spent in that particularly reserved space in the days leading to Christmas, I can only guess. In my mind a blur existed between the late medieval period and the early nineteenth century. Pages blowing fanfares from long trumpets and the spectacle of yule logs ablaze were most likely from the courtly life of the middle ages. The four-in-hand coaches, with joyous passengers and scarf-clad carolers singing beneath glowing gas light, are definitely of Dickensian vintage, standing in juxtaposition without competition. In the composite myth which is our Christmas, the one would be less without the other, for the meaning of the holiday is set in all time and in every place. Whenever and wherever its spirit of serenity and mirth are born in us, Christmas is.

Over the years I took from other sources additional powerful images and emotional evocative symbols for the Christmas season, yet remained deeply indebted to those precious cards of so long ago and the contemplative hours spent in my darkened hideaway.

# THE NIGHT WE ALMOST MISSED CHRISTMAS EVE SERVICE

## (The News Must Go Through)

*Something was extraordinarily special about the place where my father worked.*

Its importance to me is that it was here that my father, whom I greatly admired, spent his days. As a young boy, I remember it as an intriguing space filled with marvelous machinery and heavy smells, a complex maze of chambers. Such a privilege it was, to accompany my father into this most fascinating building, the town's newspaper plant.

Its immediate was the attraction of the noisy linotypes, the weighty composition tables, the rows of cabinets with large type and the lead casting box. In addition, supreme in compelling attention, was the awesome flatbed printing press, amazing in its large-scaled engineering.

Taken together, this represented the town's principal information source to the outside world. Through this enterprise were funneled, mainly by the clattering, hesitating teletypes on the second floor, the great news events of the world in the form of a newspaper.

This was also the place where my father and I would go at night in November to run off on a hand press the Christmas cards he personally had so carefully etched. During this process I was allowed to explore the recesses and mysteries of this wondrous building, as long as I did not set awry the workings of the town's crucial channel of information, its newspaper.

At that time my father was also the custodian at our family church, the First English Lutheran. In addition to cleaning the building and stoking its coal furnace, it was his duty to ring the church bell at the onset of services. This he did by pulling, with nearly his entire weigh, upon a heavy rope extending down through a small opening in the vestibule ceiling beneath the belfry. It can be well understood that to a young boy such as I this responsibility to signal the advent of worship was equal in importance to getting the news of the world out to the town.

On each Christmas Eve a hush emanated from all walls and corners of the church, as ordinary space was effused with a mystery. The air was filled with the pleasant scent of warm wax and pine and every window was appointed with candles and boughs. Every Christmas, to the right of the pulpit, stood a huge magnificent tree, simply decorated with colored lights and a bright star on top.

This was the only time in the entire liturgical year that the congregation worshipped at night, the darkness illumined by mellow light enhancing the serenity of worship.

On one particular day before Christmas, it was a raw, heavily overcast afternoon when the call came from Middlebury that the carrier could not make it to our town to pick up the papers. One might assume that this quiet, little farm town, some fourteen miles northeast from our own, could make it successfully through Christmas Day without a copy of our town's newspaper. But, that was not the way of this publisher or of my father. The news had to go through!

Thus, following a quick call to my mother, my father and I started out about five o'clock on what was to be a most unexpected adventure. With a hefty bundle of about one hundred papers secured in the trunk, my father carefully drove the company's 1941 black Studebaker coupe up the hill north of town and out into the countryside.

About halfway to our destination snow flurries began, at first just a random flake or two, but soon a dancing blanket of white appeared in the beams of the headlights. I thought, "What a wonderful gift for Christmas Eve!" Little did I know what nervous moments lay ahead.

By the time we arrived at the delivery point—a store in the town's business district, it was dark and the ground had several inches of snow. Following the delivery, we began our way home. Rather than taking the road to the west, by which we had come into town, my father chose the southern route. By that time the snow had turned to freezing rain. It was a spectacular sight, this night of gleaming ice, but now we had to concern ourselves with getting home for Christmas Eve service.

A half mile of gradual incline lay before us as we made our way toward the south. My father slowly built up speed, so as to make the grade in one attempt, taking care not to spin the wheels. (This was the time before snow tires were common and unfortunately we had no tire chains with us.) I could feel the anxiety in my father as he leaned forward over the steering wheel, peering through the ice crusted windshield. I said not a word, knowing that he was concentrating both on the sound of the tires on the ice and the possibility of staying overnight somewhere in the town.

About half way up the hill I heard the wheels begin to lose their traction, whirling more and more until we came to an agonizing stop. Undaunted, my father reversed direction, inching down the slope as he looked backward out the open door. In this second attempt to reach the summit he "gunned"—as he always called acceleration—the motor from the very start. Precariously we flew over snow and ice, like some polar express, weaving side to side. Assuming that will power could somehow propel us even further onward, we sat there emotionally straining forward. We were nearing the top! Maybe we could make it.

However, about a hundred feet from the crest of the hill the car, with the words of the paper's reliability, News-Democrat, displayed on both sides, again came to a sickening halt. How very close we had come, only to fail. We sank back distraught, hope abandoned.

After what seemed to be an interminable period of despair—actually only several real minutes—we saw far back down the hill another snow-enveloped car slowly making its way upward. Our vehicle was sitting on the lane of traffic, requiring my father to render a quick decision. He backed our car onto the side of the road, into deeper snow. There we sat dejected and not a little envious of the approaching car, which obviously had chains. A short distance behind us the car stopped and the driver got out.

Coming to my father's window the stranger said in a cheery voice, "It's a nasty night. How about a little help?" With his assistance we got our car back on the road, rocking and pushing it as we did. Once in place on the highway, this good Samaritan advanced his car until our bumpers met. With our tires spinning and his grinding, we proceeded upward to the summit. After a hearty thanks to the still anonymous gentleman, we continued on our way into the darkness of night.

The return trip was uneventful, yet nevertheless painstaking. Upon arrival at home we hastily changed into our "Sunday best," got back into the company Studebaker coupe and drove as fast as conditions permitted. Several blocks from the church we heard the first of the bell's joyous peelings. Though my dear, devoted father had missed tolling the bell—another church member had assumed the duty—we did get the papers delivered and did not miss the incomparable observance of honoring the birth of the Christ Child. The extraordinariness of Christmas Eve Candlelight Service would remain henceforth secure.

Christmas 1982
Dear Dad,

    I have sent a surprise out of the past to Fritz, one of your Christmas card etchings from the early 'Forties. I would like for you to tell your grandchildren about it, when it arrives. About how we would go uptown by evening to the News-Democrat and run the etchings off on a hand press. I wish I could be there to listen, for I think I would cherish what is said more than anyone else. They are such dear memories, the years of days before Christmas.

    This is to thank you for all the dear memories of Christmas you have given to me throughout the past. For all the Christmas trees you bought and put up for Rita and me, for the presents, from the tinker toy set to the electric train, I thank you dearly. You do know what a wonderful memory of Christmas you have given me, do you not? Were you aware of it then, that you were giving your children a love of Christmas they would never lose? That is a present that will never wear out! Out of that love of Christmas, I believe, I gave the joy of Christmas to my children. This great treasure from you shall enrich my life for as long as I shall live.

            Lovingly,
                gene

www.ingramcontent.com/pod-product-compliance
Lightning Source LLC
Chambersburg PA
CBHW041637040426
42449CB00020B/3487